MESSAGE.
MOTION.
MEASURE.

MESSAGE. MOTION. MEASURE.

A Sales Playbook for Modern Staffing and Recruiting Firms

BRIAN LILE

CONTENTS

FOREWORD

I've had the privilege of working alongside some incredibly talented professionals in the recruiting and staffing world, but few have left as lasting an impact as Brian Lile.

For nearly a decade, Brian was a key leader at our Recruitment Process Outsourcing firm, where he helped shape and scale our go-to-market strategy during a period of rapid growth. With a rare combination of strategic thinking, practical execution, and deep industry insight, Brian brought in multiple Fortune 500 clients that continue to work with us to this day.

What set Brian apart wasn't just his ability to win new business, it was *how* he did it. He built systems where there were none, created clarity in complex sales cycles, and turned prospect conversations into trusted partnerships. I watched firsthand as he developed and refined the same process he now shares in this book: **Message. Motion. Measure.**

This isn't just another sales methodology, but rather a framework forged in the trenches of real-world recruiting and designed specifically for the challenges and nuances of our industry. Brian didn't theorize this model in a vacuum; he tested it, adapted it, and delivered consistent results in one of the most competitive markets out there.

Whether you're a founder trying to scale or an individual contributor struggling to land new business, this book will give you more than tactics…it will give you direction. Brian's insights are sharp, his experience hard-earned, and his advice refreshingly actionable.

I'm proud to see the evolution of what began as field-tested strategy now shared as a guide for others. You couldn't be in better hands.

Rodney Ashby
Founder & Managing Principal, Cornerstone RPO

INTRODUCTION

If you run a small to mid-sized recruiting or staffing firm, you already know this truth: having a great service isn't enough. You might have deep industry knowledge, a strong network, or a proven ability to fill roles, but that doesn't automatically lead to a full pipeline or consistent revenue. And in today's market, it's never been harder to cut through the noise.

Prospects are overwhelmed. Budgets are under scrutiny. And your competitors are fighting for attention using the same tired playbook: vague messaging, scattered outreach, and short bursts of inconsistent activity.

The recruiting and staffing industry has changed, and if your sales strategy hasn't kept up, you're going to feel it in your pipeline, your confidence, and your bottom line.

This book is about fixing that. It's about giving you back control. It's about equipping you with a system; one built specifically for the real-world challenges firms like yours face every day. Not generic advice. Not enterprise-level theory. But a practical, proven approach that helps you connect with the right buyers, convert more meetings, and grow your firm on your terms.

Because imagine what changes when your sales process actually works:

- Your calendar fills with conversations that matter.
- Your team knows exactly what to do and why it works.
- Your firm grows with intention, not just luck.
- And you get to focus more on the work you love—delivering results—because opportunity is no longer a mystery.

If you've ever felt like your sales process wasn't quite working, or worse, that you didn't have a real process at all, you're in the right place. Because that's exactly what we're going to fix.

Throughout these pages, you'll learn the exact strategies I've used over the last 25 years to help recruiting and staffing firms build consistent, repeatable sales systems, even in tough markets. You'll walk away with a blueprint you can start implementing immediately, including:

- How to create value propositions that resonate with real buyers
- How to structure and scale your outbound activity
- What to measure in your sales funnel
- How to prepare for and run meetings that build trust
- Why momentum compounds over time and how to build it

You won't find vague motivation or one-size-fits-all templates. You'll find real strategies that are working today for firms that look just like yours.

And I'll show you how to implement it without overcomplicating your tech stack or burning out your team. Whether you're doing the work yourself, leading a small team, or thinking about getting outside help, this system is flexible and scalable.

By the end of this book, you'll have the confidence to stop guessing at what might work and start executing a strategy that actually does.

You didn't launch your firm because you wanted to become a full-time salesperson. You launched it because you're good at what you do. You help companies hire better, faster, and smarter, and you know how much value you bring when you're given the opportunity to deliver.

But the reality is this: you can't serve clients you never get the chance to meet. And without a reliable way to generate those opportunities, growth is unpredictable at best and unsustainable at worst.

The system I'll walk you through in this book is built to give you control over your sales process. Not just activity for the sake of activity, but purposeful, measurable effort that leads to consistent results. It's designed to create focus, eliminate guesswork, and build the kind of momentum that frees you up to focus on the work you care about most.

And it works. Not just for the big firms, but for the small, scrappy, service-focused companies that make up the backbone of this industry.

You don't have to figure this out on your own. You just need the right framework and the willingness to put it into play.

If you're ready to make your growth as strong as your delivery, you're exactly who this book was written for.

Let's be honest: it's easy to read a book like this, highlight a few smart ideas, and go back to business as usual. But if you've read this far, you probably know that "business as usual" isn't going to get you where you want to go, especially not in this market.

The cost of inaction isn't just lost deals. It's lost momentum. Lost confidence. A sales team that stays reactive instead of proactive. A pipeline that feels like a roller coaster. And a business that grows in fits and starts instead of scaling with consistency.

Meanwhile, your competitors are adjusting. They're clarifying their message. They're investing in strategy. They're showing up consistently in front of the same buyers you're trying to reach.

You don't have to overhaul everything overnight. But if you don't build a system—one rooted in fundamentals, driven by activity, and measured with purpose—you'll always be guessing. And guessing isn't a strategy.

This book is your opportunity to stop hoping and start executing. To stop reacting and start leading.

Because the future of your firm doesn't hinge on one big sale. It hinges on your ability to create a repeatable system that brings in the right clients, at the right time, again and again.

Let's get started.

CHAPTER 1

The Law of Supply & Demand

"You can't repeal the law of supply and demand — even if you're Congress."
— Ronald Reagan

A Crowded, Contracting Market

Let's start with the truth: there are nearly **26,000 staffing and recruiting firms** in the U.S. as of 2025. That includes everything from temp agencies to boutique search firms to RPO providers. And all of them are fighting for their share of a market that's shrunk by **24% since 2022.**

Now layer in this: your competitors aren't just other firms. You're also competing against your clients' internal recruiting teams, many of which have been told to "bring it in-house" as a cost-saving strategy.

You've heard the phrase before. "We've decided to build our internal team." Or the slightly softer version: "We're only using agencies for hard-to-fill roles." Either way, it lands the same — your pipeline just took a hit.

And if you're like most firm owners I talk to, you're not just feeling the market pressure. You're watching long-standing clients pull back, asking for reduced rates, longer terms, or just disappearing entirely.

So, how did we get here?

What's Driving the Decline

Over the last three years, the recruiting and staffing market has been hit from multiple directions:

- **Economic uncertainty** fueled by inflation concerns and recession fears
- **Geopolitical instability** and regulatory unpredictability
- **A weakened manufacturing sector** and slowing demand in key verticals
- **Tighter budgets** leading to delayed or cancelled hiring plans
- **More procurement oversight**, legal review, and red tape
- **Shifting worker preferences**, favoring permanent roles over temporary ones

Even when clients *are* hiring, they're cautious. They scrutinize every cost. They're under pressure to justify spend and reduce reliance on outside vendors. And recruiting services, fair or not, are often seen as discretionary in these moments.

The result? Fewer deals. Lower margins. Longer sales cycles. And in many cases, silence on the other end of your outreach.

You're Not Alone in This

If you're struggling to generate new business right now, you're not the only one. I've had countless conversations with firm owners who feel like they're doing everything right and still coming up short.

They've invested in tools. Hired great people. Built service offerings they're proud of. But the market just isn't responding like it used to. Clients are slower to make decisions. Prospects are harder to reach. And even when there's interest, the path from first touch to signed agreement feels longer than ever.

Worse, many of these owners are losing faith in their messaging, in their value, even in themselves.

And it's not just about economics. It's emotional. Because when you know your work brings value, but no one's listening, it's easy to start questioning everything.

Let's pause here, because this part often goes unsaid.

-It's not just about lost deals. It's the weight you carry between calls, wondering if you're doing something wrong, or if the industry is just broken. It's the nagging voice at 2 a.m. when you're staring at the ceiling, asking yourself if you're falling behind. It's opening your CRM and feeling defeated by the silence. It's the pressure of payroll with no new revenue in sight.

This isn't just business stress. It bleeds into your mood, your relationships, and your health. You get shorter with your team.

Less present at home. You start thinking smaller, playing it safer, because hope starts to feel expensive.

If that sounds familiar, you're not broken. And you're definitely not alone.

We've Been Here Before — And We've Gotten Through It

This isn't the first time our industry has hit a wall. If you've been in staffing long enough, you've seen this pattern: sharp downturns followed by slow, uneven recoveries.

Here are three that reshaped the industry:

The Dot-Com Bust (2000–2002)

The NASDAQ lost nearly 80% of its value. Tech companies collapsed. The staffing industry saw a **30–40% drop in revenue**, especially in IT and telecom.

The Great Recession (2008–2010)

Triggered by the housing and financial crisis, this downturn led to **a 30%+ drop in staffing employment** in just one year (2009).

The COVID-19 Crash (2020)

The shutdowns were sudden and brutal. Staffing **revenues dropped 11%**, and temporary staffing demand evaporated in Q2, although healthcare and remote-friendly sectors rebounded faster.

Every one of these periods tested the industry and the people in it. But we made it through.

Each of these downturns taught us something.

During the Dot-Com Bust, the firms that survived were the ones that quickly diversified their client base. Tech was imploding, but other industries still needed talent. Those who reacted fast found new revenue.

In the Great Recession, we saw the rise of contract staffing as a cost-containment tool. Clients still had needs but wanted flexibility. Firms that adapted their offering and got creative with pricing and terms found ways to stay relevant.

And during COVID, the firms that leaned into digital transformation were the first to bounce back. Those who waited, hoping for a return to "normal," got left behind.

In each case, the lesson was clear: adapt quickly, focus deeply, and never wait for the market to fix itself.

You don't control the conditions. But you do control your response.

A Real Example: How One Firm Found Stability in the Storm

Let me introduce you to Claire, the founder of a six-person staffing firm focused on operations roles in mid-market manufacturing. Like many in early 2023, her pipeline slowed to a trickle. Two of her top clients froze hiring. Another asked for a 25% rate reduction. Her usual cadence of warm leads went cold.

She was burning through cash, working nights, and questioning whether she could keep her team together.

When we started working together, Claire wasn't lacking hustle; she was lacking focus. She was trying to be everything to everyone. Her messaging was generic, and her outreach scattered. She had a CRM full of contacts but no clear plan for how to engage them.

We started by getting hyper-specific. She chose a vertical where she had strong placements and client stories: food and beverage manufacturing. Then we rebuilt her value propositions around one clear pain point: reducing the cost of a bad hire in a labor-constrained environment.

Next, we mapped out an outbound rhythm with blended outreach methods. Every step of the process was tied back to her value story, backed by examples.

Within six weeks, Claire had re-engaged two old prospects and landed a new retained search with a midwestern food producer—at full rate. Her confidence returned. Her team got realigned. And most importantly, she wasn't waking up in the middle of the night worried about cash flow.

She didn't wait for the market to get easier. She built a system that worked anyway.

And so can you.

The Weight of Uncertainty

Here's what makes this moment different: the market isn't just tough, it's confusing. You don't know what's coming next. And that makes it hard to plan.

Do you double down on your current strategy? Invest in new tools? Pivot to a new vertical? Train your team or outsource more of the work? Do you pull back entirely?

Those are fair questions. And in the chapters that follow, I'm going to help you answer them.

But before we start talking tactics, we need to acknowledge what this pressure does to you as a business owner. It wears you down. It makes you second-guess yourself. And in some cases, it makes you pull back right when you need to push forward.

That pressure creates doubt. Doubt in your positioning. Doubt in your team. Doubt in your own ability to turn things around.

But here's the truth: most firm owners aren't trained in sales strategy. You're a recruiter. A builder. A connector. Sales became your job when you became the boss—and no one handed you a playbook.

That means your current results aren't a reflection of your value. They're a reflection of your system—or the lack of one.

And that's what we're going to fix.

My Story — and Why I'm Sharing This With You

I've spent the last 25 years in this industry. I've sold in boom years and in brutal years. I've sat across the table from skeptical clients and unsure decision-makers more times than I can count.

I've had great quarters. I've missed quotas. I've been confident, and I've been humbled.

But through it all, I kept learning. I studied what worked — and what didn't. I focused on building a strategy that would hold up no matter the market conditions. And over time, I developed a system that helped me generate new business predictably, even when the industry was struggling.

And here's where we turn the corner.

You can't solve a problem you're too overwhelmed to look at clearly. That's what this first chapter is about: naming the problem. Staring it down. Understanding the forces that are working against you—so you can stop fighting shadows and start fighting strategically.

In the next chapter, we begin building. We shift from reactive to proactive. From scattered effort to focused action.

Because it's time to stop letting the market dictate your outcomes—and start designing a system that works no matter what it throws your way.

Eventually, that system became the foundation of my consulting practice. Now I work with firm owners across the country, helping them build real sales strategy, not just activity.

This book is your front-row seat to that system.

CHAPTER 2

The Tough Sell

When I first started in the staffing industry, I thought the hard part would be finding candidates. Turns out, that was the easy part.

The real challenge? Selling the service.

At the time, I didn't have much formal sales training. I wasn't a natural extrovert. I didn't thrive on cold calls or live for objections. I was fresh out of college and quickly found myself dialing into offices, interrupting busy professionals who didn't know me and definitely weren't expecting my pitch.

To make matters worse, the industry was reeling from the Dot-Com crash. Tech companies were folding. Clients were tightening their budgets. Then, just one month into my new role, the world changed on September 11th. Uncertainty took over everything: business, markets, the economy, even our daily lives.

In many ways, it was a brutal introduction to the business. But it also forced me to learn quickly not just how to sell, but how to survive in a market where the margin for error was razor thin.

Why Selling Recruiting & Staffing Services Feels So Hard

If you're struggling to get traction right now — to generate meetings, move deals forward, or stand out in a crowded space — you're not alone. The truth is, this industry presents a unique combination of challenges that make selling difficult, even for seasoned professionals.

Let's take a closer look.

You're Selling an Intangible Service

Unlike a product demo or software free trial, you can't hand your prospect something to try out. You can't show them a sleek interface or give them a 14-day test run. What you're selling is a promise that your firm will deliver the right people, at the right time, in a way that justifies the investment.

That's hard to prove in a first conversation. It's even harder when they've been burned before.

Trust Isn't Optional — and It Doesn't Come Fast

In recruiting and staffing, trust isn't a nice-to-have, it's everything. Your client is betting their time, their reputation, and sometimes their team's performance on your ability to deliver. That's a big ask, and most decision-makers don't offer trust quickly.

This is why sales cycles in our industry are long. It's not because we don't explain our value, it's because our value can't be fully seen until well after the deal is signed. And in uncertain markets, trust becomes even harder to earn.

It All Sounds the Same to Them

You might know how your firm is different. But if your messaging sounds anything like, "We have great candidates, deep networks, and a fast turnaround," then your prospects are hearing the same pitch they've heard ten times this week.

We all say we're different. But if your value proposition doesn't speak directly to the outcomes your buyer cares about, you'll blend right in with the noise. (We'll dive deeper into how to fix this in Chapter 5.)

The Buying Process Is Messy

You're not selling to one person, you're selling to a committee. And often, the people involved in the decision have conflicting priorities or limited visibility into the actual value of your service.

You might have a great conversation with a hiring manager who sees the need, but they're not the final decision-maker. Or you might get support from HR, only to hit a wall with Finance or Procurement. It's a maze. And without a clear strategy to navigate it, deals stall out fast.

The Stakes Are High

Your buyer is putting their credibility on the line by bringing in an outside vendor. If you miss, if your candidates fall short or your process underdelivers, they take the heat.

That pressure often leads to hesitation, second-guessing, and delays. The higher the perceived risk, the slower the decision-making process becomes. You're not just managing a sales funnel, you're managing fear, reputation, and internal politics.

When you step back and look at all of this together, it's no wonder that even talented, experienced firm owners struggle with sales.

Cold Outreach, Meet the Ice Age

Now, let's layer in the current reality: everyone is doing outreach, and prospects have stopped responding.

With over 26,000 staffing and recruiting firms in the U.S., your ideal client is getting bombarded from every angle. It's not just you. It's inboxes that are flooded with pitches, LinkedIn DMs, cold calls, and "just checking in" follow-ups.

But here's the kicker — traditional channels don't work like they used to.

Take email. It used to be one of the most effective tools in our sales process. You could write a short, direct message and book a meeting with someone you couldn't reach by phone.

Not anymore.

Your message is now competing with vendor noise, internal fire drills, calendar invites, newsletters, and spam. On average, over **122 billion** spam messages are sent every day. Most professionals receive **10–50 spam emails** a day, and that number only grows the longer their email account has been active.

The result? Email providers have clamped down. Spam filters are smarter. Engagement scoring is tougher. And even personalized, well-written emails frequently get pushed into junk or promotion folders.

Now add automation. AI-powered outreach tools have made it easier than ever for *everyone* to blast messages at scale, which means your prospect is seeing the same formats, the same templates, and the same tone over and over again.

Even if your message is good, it looks like all the rest.

And while we'll talk more about outreach strategies and channels in a later chapter, one thing is clear: breaking through has never been harder.

The Robots Showed Up — And They're Not Slowing Down

If that weren't enough, we now face a new challenge: AI isn't just changing how we sell, it's changing what our clients believe they need from us.

This shift is already happening.

Tools like HireEZ, SeekOut, and LinkedIn Recruiter AI can now source thousands of candidates in seconds. Screening platforms like Pymetrics, Harver, and Modern Hire use AI to assess fit, run evaluations, and even conduct first-round interviews. And more companies are building internal talent marketplaces to redeploy existing employees instead of hiring new ones.

This means fewer open roles. Fewer outsourced searches. And more clients questioning why they need an external partner at all.

We can argue about the effectiveness of these tools, and there's plenty to debate. But for the buyer, AI offers something very appealing: speed, perceived control, and cost savings.

And if your positioning is based purely on process, turnaround time, or database depth? You're competing with a machine. The "easy money" is drying up. The middle-of-the-funnel business is evaporating. To stay relevant, you have to show value that *AI can't replicate.*

That means insights. Strategy. Trusted partnership. Judgment.

And all of that begins with *how* you sell, not just *what* you sell.

Why This Chapter Matters

You need to understand what you're really up against — not to feel discouraged, but to get clear-eyed about what it's going to take to win.

This is not a normal market. This is not a time for half-measures. And this is not a sale that happens by accident.

But here's the good news: once you understand the challenges, you can plan for them and outmaneuver them through strategy.

That's what this book is about – building a sales system that works *because* it's designed for markets like this one.

CHAPTER 3

The Consequences of Inaction

"Half measures are the curse of mediocrity."
— Unknown

Half Measures, Whole Problems

One of the most common patterns I see when working with small recruiting and staffing firms is a reluctance to fully commit to a focused sales strategy. Instead, the sales process ends up as a patchwork of half-hearted efforts: an outdated pitch deck here, a couple of blog posts from years ago, a LinkedIn post once a month, maybe an email tool that no one really knows how to use anymore.

And the CRM? If it's even being used, it's usually full of stale leads, unclear next steps, and no reliable way to track real-time progress.

This isn't about blame. In fact, it's completely understandable.

When business was booming, there wasn't much pressure to overhaul your sales process. Referrals came in. Repeat clients stayed loyal. Margins were strong enough to mask inefficiencies. You were busy doing what you do best — serving clients, managing delivery, and putting out the daily fires that come with running a company.

But what used to be optional — a defined sales strategy, consistent messaging, and pipeline visibility — has now become the baseline requirement to stay competitive.

In today's market, doing "just enough" doesn't just lead to slower growth. It leads to stalled pipelines, lost ground, and a creeping sense of frustration that's hard to shake.

If this sounds familiar, you're not alone, but now is the time to face it head-on.

When 'Later' Becomes 'Too Late'

When the market slows down, it's natural to go into conservation mode. Cut costs. Tighten up. Hold your breath until things settle.

But here's what doesn't show up on your P&L: the cost of doing nothing.

Inaction doesn't just pause growth. It erodes momentum quietly. It looks like a sales team that stops following up. A prospect that loses interest. A pitch that hasn't been updated since 2019. A website that still says "best-in-class candidates" and "exceptional service" — just like everyone else's.

Let's talk about what that really costs you.

Opportunity Loss

Deals don't just fall through because of bad timing. Often, they slip away because no one followed up. Because the message didn't resonate. Because the buyer didn't feel any urgency and the seller didn't create any.

In this market, your prospects still buy. But they buy from firms that show up consistently, speak to their pain points, and build trust over time. Without a strategy, your team becomes reactive — and that's when good opportunities quietly walk out the door.

Pipeline Decay

Here's something most firm owners underestimate: pipelines rot.

If your CRM is full of contacts who haven't heard from you in weeks, or worse, months, those deals aren't "in progress." They're fading.

Without a structured cadence to move conversations forward, even warm leads cool quickly. And when leadership has no visibility into what's actually happening in the funnel, the data becomes misleading. What looks like a full pipeline is often just a graveyard of stale opportunities.

Brand Damage

Your buyers don't just hear your words — they absorb your presence (or lack thereof). When your sales effort feels scattered, inconsistent, or outdated, that reflects on your firm. Your outreach blends in. Your positioning feels vague. And even if your delivery is strong, your first impression is weak.

That perception matters. Because in a crowded market, forgettable equals replaceable.

And the hardest part? None of this feels urgent until it is.

You don't feel the weight of lost deals because they're invisible. You don't notice the rep who's mentally checked out. You don't see the growth that could've happened until your competitor shows up in a place you should've been.

That's the hidden cost of inaction. And it's the reason "wait and see" is rarely the right call.

Moving Forward Starts Now

If any of this feels familiar — the outdated messaging, the neglected CRM, the missed follow-ups, the cold outreach that goes nowhere — you're in good company. These aren't isolated issues. They're industry-wide. I've worked with firms of all sizes, and I've seen the same patterns play out again and again.

It's not a reflection of your capability. It's a reflection of a market that changed faster than most people expected and a system that was never built for what we're facing now.

But the good news? It's not too late to fix it.

I've spent the last 25 years in this business. I started out on the phones during one of the worst hiring climates in modern history. I've sold through recessions, downturns, and Black Swan events. I've made the mistakes you've made. I've ignored leads. I've relied on referrals too long. I've assumed that what worked last year would still work today.

Eventually, I stopped hoping the market would come back and started building a system that worked no matter what the market was doing.

That's the system I'm going to walk you through in the chapters ahead.

This isn't theory or a sales methodology pulled from a Fortune 500 boardroom. This is a ground-level, field-tested framework that's helped small recruiting and staffing firms regain control of their pipeline, clarify their message, and start closing business again.

But before we get into the how, I need to make something clear:

This won't work if you're still waiting for things to "normalize." There is no normal coming back. There's only what's next, and whether or not you're ready for it.

What We'll Cover From Here

In the next chapters, I'm going to show you exactly how to rebuild your sales strategy, piece by piece, to reflect what's actually working right now in our industry.

We'll talk about how to develop messaging that actually lands, messaging that connects with real buyer pain points and differentiates you from the dozens of other firms saying the same thing. We'll get into how to scale your outreach the right way, increasing volume without turning your brand into spam.

You'll learn how to use your sales funnel as a tool for decision-making and how to uncover what's really moving deals forward (or holding them back).

I'll walk you through how to prepare for prospect meetings with purpose, lead the conversation, and position yourself as a trusted partner, not just another vendor in their inbox.

And finally, we'll talk about consistency. Because in this market, the firms that win aren't the ones with the best pitch. They're the ones who keep showing up with the right message to the right people at the right pace.

You don't need to be perfect. You just need to get serious about fixing what's broken and commit to showing up with intent.

No More Half Measures

If you're still reading this, you've already cleared the first hurdle: you're paying attention. That alone sets you apart.

Most staffing and recruiting firm owners know something isn't working, but they keep throwing time, tools, or hope at the problem instead of stepping back and asking: *What's the system we're actually running? And is it built for the market we're in or the market we wish we had?*

The chapters ahead are going to help you answer that. More importantly, they're going to help you fix it.

The work won't always be easy. Change rarely is. But it's doable. And more than that, it's necessary.

Because the market's not going to wait. And neither should you.

Let's get to work.

CHAPTER 4

Message. Motion. Measure.

"Complexity is the enemy of execution."
— Tony Robbins

By now, you know what's not working — the scattered outreach, the inconsistent effort, the outdated messaging, and the silence that follows. The good news? There's a way forward. It's not a silver bullet or a 10-step hack. It's a system — simple, focused, and built to do exactly what many firms in this industry fail to do: create consistent, repeatable sales results.

Since starting my consulting practice, I've helped many small staffing and recruiting firms cut through the noise, stop guessing, and start selling with purpose. And no matter the market, the vertical, or the economic climate, I keep coming back to the same three pillars that drive real progress: **Message. Motion. Measure.**

These three elements work together like gears in a machine. You need all three in sync. Not one, not two. Just one missing piece, and the entire system breaks down.

Message is about clarity. Developing value propositions that actually resonate with the specific people you're trying to reach. Not generic promises, but targeted language that speaks directly to the priorities, pressures, and pain points of your buyer personas.

Motion is about doing the work. Increasing the volume of outreach and sales activity to a level that gives you a real shot at generating opportunities. Hope is not a strategy. Momentum comes from movement, and most firms are operating well below the level of effort required to succeed in today's market.

Measure is about feedback. Measuring what's working, what's not, and making adjustments until the formula clicks. This is where strategy becomes science. Without numbers, you're flying blind. With them, you're building a repeatable process that scales.

In the chapters that follow, I'm going to walk you through each of these principles — not just what they mean, but how to apply them, how to troubleshoot them, and how to build them into the foundation of your business.

No more wishful thinking. No more waiting around for leads to appear. It's time to get serious. Because if you get the message right, put in the motion, and track the right metrics, you will see results.

Message.

Most staffing and recruiting firms think they have a messaging problem, but what they really have is a *relevance* problem. Their value propositions are generic, vague, or worse — designed to appeal to everyone. And when you try to speak to everyone, you end up resonating with no one.

Effective messaging starts with one simple principle: talk to the person who's reading it. Not the company. Not the industry. The *person*. That means you need to understand your buyer personas — who they are, what they care about, what pressures they're under, and what outcomes they're trying to deliver.

A VP of HR at a large healthcare system isn't thinking about the same things as a plant manager in a midsize manufacturing company. A CFO isn't going to respond to the same message that works for a Director of Talent Acquisition. Yet time and again, I see some iteration of "We provide high-quality candidates quickly through our proven process," which says everything and nothing at the same time.

When your messaging fails to connect with your buyer's specific world, it gets ignored. Or worse, it gets deleted before it's even opened.

This doesn't mean you need to write a completely different pitch for every prospect. But it *does* mean you need to build messaging tracks that align with each of your core buyer personas —messages that speak directly to their role, their goals, and their pain points.

That's where we start, with message clarity. Because if your prospects don't feel like you understand them, they'll never believe you can help them.

Motion.

Once you've clarified what you're saying, the next step is simple: say it — a lot. This is where most firms fall flat. They assume that once they've got their message figured out, a few emails, a couple of LinkedIn posts, and a call or two will be enough to generate opportunities.

It won't be.

In today's market, volume is critical. Buyers are distracted, overwhelmed, and busier than ever. Even if your message is great, you're still competing with hundreds of other voices — internal emails, vendor pitches, industry noise, and personal obligations. Getting their attention once is hard. Earning enough of it to start a conversation takes consistent, high-frequency outreach.

If you think you're doing enough, you probably aren't. Most small firms dramatically underestimate the volume of sales activity required to create real momentum. I've worked with clients who were reaching out to 20 people a week and wondering why they weren't seeing results. When we increased that to a couple hundred relevant contacts per week, across phone, email, LinkedIn, and other contact methods, conversations started happening. Pipelines grew. Deals started moving.

This doesn't mean "spray and pray." It means purposeful, high-volume activity — guided by strong messaging, targeting the right personas, and executed with consistency week after week.

Motion is about discipline. It's about putting in the reps, even when you're not getting immediate responses. It's about understanding that momentum in sales is earned, not handed out.

You don't need to burn yourself out, burn out your team, or build a call center. But you do need to increase your effort to a level that gives your strategy a chance to work. In this industry, hope is not a pipeline, and occasional effort is not a plan.

When message and motion work together, you start to generate traction. And when you combine that with data, that's when the real leverage appears.

Measure.

If *message* gives you direction, and *motion* creates momentum, then *measure* is what keeps you on course. Without data, even the best sales strategy is just a guess, and guessing is a luxury no one in this industry can afford right now.

One of the biggest issues I see with staffing and recruiting firms is a total lack of visibility into what's actually happening in their sales efforts. Outreach is happening (maybe), but no one's tracking how much, to whom, through which channels, or with what result. And when deals stall or leads dry up, there's no way to know *why*, or what to do about it.

Measuring changes that.

Tracking the right sales metrics gives you the feedback loop you need to adjust, refine, and scale. It tells you whether your message is landing, whether your outreach volume is enough, and whether your team is spending time in the right places — or just staying busy without moving the needle.

You don't need a wall of dashboards to make progress. What you need is consistency. Numbers you trust. A rhythm of weekly reviews. And the discipline to act on what the data tells you, even if it means making changes you didn't want to make.

Sales isn't just art. It's also science. And if you aren't measuring, you're guessing. When you start measuring, you unlock real leverage. You can identify what's working and double down. You can spot problems early and fix them before they cost you a quarter. And most importantly, you can build a sales system that's not dependent on luck, timing, or one rainmaker carrying the whole load.

This is how real sales performance is built — through message, motion, and measuring. Together, they form the foundation of everything we'll build from here.

From Principles to Practice

Message. Motion. Measure.

These three pillars form the foundation of any successful sales strategy — especially in a tough, noisy market like the one we're navigating today. If you've been struggling with inconsistent results, stalled deals, or a sales process that just feels stuck, it almost always comes back to one (or more) of these areas being out of alignment. In the chapters ahead, we're going to dig into each topic and I'll show you how I apply these principles to sell recruiting and staffing services.

You'll learn how to build targeted value propositions that resonate with the specific buyer personas you're selling to, not vague, one-size-fits-all messaging, but real positioning that cuts through the noise.

We'll look at how to scale outreach in a way that's intentional, consistent, and sustainable, without burning yourself or your team out. I'll show you what the right level of sales activity actually looks like and how to increase volume without sacrificing quality.

Then we'll dive into metrics — what to track, how to interpret it, and how to use it to drive real decisions. You'll learn how to build a feedback loop into your sales process that helps you optimize over time instead of running in circles.

And finally, we'll walk through how to prepare for and run a sales meeting, the kind that actually moves deals forward, builds trust with your buyers, and increases your close rate.

You don't need a flashy tech stack or a massive sales team to make this work. You need focus. You need structure. And you need to execute on the fundamentals that matter most.

Let's get to it.

CHAPTER 5

The Right Words Can Change Everything

"Differentiate or die."
— Jack Trout

Most staffing firms believe they're delivering something unique, but few can explain it in a way that actually lands with a buyer. You can have the best recruiting team, the most efficient process, and a track record of great placements, but if your message sounds like everyone else's, buyers will treat you like everyone else. In a market this saturated, how you talk about your value matters as much as the value itself.

The good news? Differentiation is possible, even in an industry where everyone claims the same things. But it takes focus, discipline, and a clear understanding of your audience.

In this chapter, we're going to dig into the real-world mechanics of building a strong value proposition, one that doesn't just describe what you do, but connects to what your buyer actually *cares about*. We'll start by breaking down the myth of differentiation and looking at why most messaging fails to stand out. Then we'll explore how to define and prioritize your core buyer personas, the key players you need to influence. Finally, we'll put it all together and walk through how to craft value propositions that are specific, relevant, and hard to ignore.

Because the firms that win in this market aren't necessarily better, they're just *clearer*.

Let's sharpen your message.

Proof Beats Promises

Ask any staffing firm what makes them different, and you'll hear the same responses over and over again: "We have a great network." "We move fast." "We really understand our clients." It's not that those things aren't true, it's that every other firm says the exact same thing. And when everyone is claiming the same strengths, nothing actually stands out.

Here's the hard truth: your prospective clients don't believe what you say, they believe what you've done. That's why one of the most effective ways to differentiate your firm is to lead with past results.

Results provide credibility. They shift the conversation from generic claims to proven impact. When you can show a prospect that you helped a similar company reduce time-to-fill by 40%, or saved a client $150K by reducing turnover, you're not just selling staffing, you're offering a business outcome.

This doesn't mean you need flashy case studies with logos and polished graphics (although those can help). It means being able to clearly tell stories about who you've helped, what the challenge was, and what happened as a result. Real examples that reflect the problems your prospects are wrestling with right now.

And here's where the differentiation sharpens: the more tailored your examples are to the buyer's world, the more powerful they become. If you're talking to a Director of Talent Acquisition in healthcare, and you can point to success with another healthcare client, especially around something that director also cares about, like candidate experience or fill ratios, your value instantly becomes more believable.

If your firm is relatively new or hasn't tracked results in a formal way, start by capturing even small wins. Use before-and-after metrics. Tell the story of how a client went from struggling to hire to finally building momentum. It's not about bragging, it's about giving your prospect confidence that you can deliver.

This is one of the first things I work on with my clients: identifying the success stories they've already created and turning them into messaging that opens doors. Most firms have plenty of wins, they just haven't learned how to use them as proof points in a way that resonates with their ideal buyers.

You don't need to invent a new process or be the flashiest firm in the market to stand out. You just need to demonstrate that you've done what your buyer is trying to do, and that you can do it again.

Because in this industry, proof beats promises every time.

Right Story for the Right Person

One of the most common mistakes I see in recruiting and staffing sales is the belief that one value proposition can work for everyone. It's understandable — your firm likely offers a single core service: finding great talent. But the mistake isn't in *what you do*, it's in how you *talk about it.*

Because different buyers care about different things.

The priorities of a CFO are not the same as a VP of HR. A regional operations leader isn't focused on the same challenges as a Director of Talent Acquisition. And if you're sending the same message to all of them, or worse, crafting messaging without knowing *who* it's for, you're missing the mark before the conversation even starts.

That's why defining your buyer personas is a critical step in crafting compelling value propositions. A buyer persona is more than a job title. It's a profile that includes what that person is responsible for, what metrics they're judged by, what challenges they face, and how your service intersects with their goals and pain points.

When you know who you're talking to, you can speak their language.

For example, a CFO may be concerned with labor cost containment and ROI, so your message should focus on cost savings, workforce flexibility, and risk mitigation. Meanwhile, a Director of HR may be more focused on candidate quality, compliance, or retention, so your value proposition should highlight efficiency, reduced turnover, and cultural fit.

The better your personas, the more relevant your messaging. And relevance is what earns attention.

This is where I spend a lot of time with my clients. Helping them identify their key buyer personas and mapping their messaging to each one. Once you have clarity on who your real buyers are and what matters to them, the rest of your sales messaging becomes significantly easier and more effective.

You don't need ten different personas to start. Focus on the top three or four types of buyers you sell to most often. Define their role, their goals, and what a successful partnership looks like from *their* point of view. Then build your messaging around that.

Because the key to making your value proposition land isn't just in what you say, it's in *who* you say it to, and how clearly it speaks to *them*.

Win Again with What Worked Before

When it comes time to build value propositions that actually resonate, most firms overthink it. They brainstorm clever taglines, debate wording endlessly, or try to invent something that sounds different instead of starting with the most obvious and powerful source of value they already have:

Their current clients.

If you've helped a client solve a meaningful hiring problem, reduce time-to-fill, improve retention, or scale quickly, you already have a value proposition. You just need to capture it and position it the right way.

One of the most effective ways to build a sales campaign is to take what's working for your current clients and use that success story to prospect their competitors. You're not just saying, "Here's what we do." You're saying, "Here's what we did for a company just like yours and here's how we can do it for you."

This strategy instantly boosts credibility. It removes a layer of risk from the buyer's mind. It shows that your firm understands their industry, their challenges, and their priorities because you've already helped someone in their world succeed.

I recommend this approach often when helping clients build new campaigns: identify one client success story with a compelling result, extract the core outcomes (quantifiable when possible), and shape that story into a message to share with their competitors. This doesn't just make your outreach more effective, it makes it easier to scale.

The key is to frame the story around the buyer's perspective, not your own. Don't just say, "We placed 15 roles in 90 days." Say, "We helped a company in [industry] reduce time-to-fill by 35% in one quarter, helping them hit a critical production milestone with no delays." That's not a brag, that's a result. And results are what buyers respond to.

When you do this consistently, you build a library of mini case studies that you can plug into campaigns by role, by industry, or by use case. These become the building blocks of your go-to-market strategy: specific, relevant, and proven.

Your goal isn't to sound different for the sake of it. Your goal is to prove that your firm creates real outcomes and that you've done it for companies just like the ones you're reaching out to.

That's how you turn value into traction and start the right conversations. And that's how you make your message impossible to ignore.

Case Study: Messaging That Cut Through the Noise

Maya ran a boutique staffing firm that specialized in technical placements for logistics and supply chain companies. Her team was solid, her placements were strong, and her client retention was excellent — but new business had all but stalled.

Her messaging sounded just like everyone else's: "We're fast, we understand your business, we have a great network." She was frustrated. "We actually are different," she said. "But I don't know how to say it in a way that makes people pay attention."

We started by identifying her top three buyer personas: COOs, HR Directors, and Plant Managers at midsize logistics companies. For each, we mapped their goals and frustrations. Then we reviewed past placements and found a pattern: her firm had helped several clients cut overtime spending by reducing time-to-fill — a metric that mattered deeply to operations and HR leaders.

We rewrote her value proposition to lead with this outcome: "We help logistics firms reduce overtime costs by filling technical roles 40% faster than the industry average without sacrificing quality." It was specific, relevant, and backed by real results.

The change was immediate. Her outbound messages started getting replies. She booked six prospect calls in two weeks, more than she'd booked in the previous four months. One prospect even said, "I get messages from staffing companies every day. This is the first one I've read all the way through."

By aligning her message to what her buyers actually cared about, and proving she'd done it before, Maya turned vague claims into compelling proof.

And that clarity created momentum.

Words to Wins

If you've been struggling to stand out, unsure how to explain your value, or frustrated that prospects just don't seem to "get it," it's not because your service isn't strong, it's because your message hasn't been sharp enough. The firms that succeed in today's market aren't always the biggest or flashiest. They're the ones who know how to say the right thing to the right person at the right time.

Differentiation doesn't come from clever slogans or sweeping claims. It comes from proof. From relevance. From showing a prospect that you understand their world and that you've already helped someone just like them succeed.

That's what a strong value proposition does. It doesn't just tell a story. It tells *their* story, with you in the role of trusted partner, not desperate vendor.

In the next chapter, we're going to keep building. Because a strong message is powerful but it's just the beginning. Next, we'll talk about how to get our improved messaging in front of our prospects at the scale required to generate results.

Because while clarity can get you in the door, you still have to knock on a LOT of doors.

CHAPTER 6

Reps Build Results

"Volume negates luck."
— Alex Hormozi

If you've ever started a new fitness routine, you know that doing a few workouts here and there doesn't move the needle. You can't just go for a jog twice a week and expect to see real change. The people who make progress, who actually get stronger, leaner, or healthier, are the ones who show up consistently and put in enough reps to make a difference.

The same principle applies to sales.

Most recruiting and staffing firms drastically underestimate the volume of activity needed to generate consistent results. They send a few emails, make a couple of calls, post on LinkedIn now and then, and then wonder why their calendars are empty and their pipeline is dry.

The truth is, the market is noisier, harder to penetrate, and more skeptical than ever. If you want results, you need more than just a strong message. You need **motion**, the kind that creates momentum.

This chapter is about the effort behind the outcomes: how many touches it actually takes to create conversations, what kind of volume is realistic in today's environment, and how the most effective firms build the stamina to stay visible without burning out.

We'll also talk about how to use automation tools to help you increase your activity without losing your mind, and how to stay aligned with your targeted buyer personas while keeping your outreach engine running.

Because in this market, volume isn't optional.

The Outreach Gap

One of the most common patterns I see when talking to staffing firm owners is this: they're frustrated with the lack of meetings, stuck with a quiet calendar, and convinced something must be wrong with their message. And while that is usually the case, they have another problem: they're not talking to enough people.

The single biggest miscalculation most firms make is underestimating the sheer number of leads they need to contact to generate meaningful activity.

In a looser market, you might be able to get by with reaching out to 20 or 30 people a week. You could count on a few warm intros, a couple of referrals, maybe even some inbound interest. But those days are behind us. Today's market is tighter, more cautious, and flooded with vendors all offering some version of the same pitch.

So here's the hard truth: you have to do a lot more than you think just to find the companies that are actually in a buying posture.

Outreach isn't about convincing everyone; it's about *finding the few* who are ready for help. And that takes scale. You have to cast a wider net to uncover the right opportunities. That means contacting dozens —even hundreds — of leads each week, not as a one-time campaign, but as a sustained part of your sales process.

This is where many teams fall short. They treat outreach like a project instead of a system. They make 20 calls, send 40 emails, and assume they've done their part. But when those numbers don't produce results, it's not because they're doing something wrong, it's because they're not doing enough.

And this isn't about working harder, it's about working at the right scale.

When I work with clients, one of the first adjustments we make is increasing activity levels, often by 3x to 5x. Not with random blasting, but with intentional, persona-aligned outreach that's delivered at a frequency that gives it a real chance to land. Once the volume is there, everything else becomes easier: better response rates, clearer patterns, more meetings.

You cannot afford to wait for leads to appear. You have to go find them. And in today's market, that means doing more than feels comfortable, more than you're used to, and more than your competitors are willing to do consistently.

Because right now, the firms that are winning aren't necessarily better, they're just putting in more reps.

Scaling Smart

Once you understand the level of activity required to generate real results, the next question becomes: *How do I actually do that without burning out or blowing up my day?* The answer is leverage, and for outbound sales, that means using automation tools to increase your reach without sacrificing quality.

In today's market, you simply can't hit the numbers manually. If you're trying to build momentum one email or one LinkedIn message at a time, you'll fall behind before you even start. That's why automation, when used the right way, is a game-changer.

There are tools that can help you automate large parts of your email and LinkedIn outreach. You can build personalized, multi-step sequences that send over time. You can schedule follow-ups, test different messaging tracks, and even adjust cadence based on engagement. The best tools make it feel like a human is behind every touchpoint, even if you're reaching hundreds of people.

That said, automation is not a silver bullet. It doesn't work without strategy, and it doesn't excuse lazy messaging. It only works if you've done the work to define your buyer personas, craft compelling value propositions, and build thoughtful campaigns. But once you have that in place, automation lets you scale without letting anything fall through the cracks.

You may remember from an earlier chapter that email isn't as effective as it once was, and that's still true. Spam filters are tighter. Inboxes are overloaded. But email hasn't stopped working altogether — it just can't do the job on its own anymore.

The modern outreach strategy is multi-channel. Email alone is incomplete. LinkedIn alone is slow. Cold calls alone are inefficient. But when you combine email automation, LinkedIn messaging, and phone outreach into a cohesive system, you increase your surface area and your odds of starting meaningful conversations.

This is where I help many of my clients find traction. We take the refined messaging we've created and layer in automation tools to increase volume across multiple channels, all while staying aligned with their target personas.

Automation won't *replace* the effort, but it *multiplies* the effort.

Precision at Scale

By now, you understand that more activity is non-negotiable. But let's be clear: this isn't about doing more for the sake of doing more. It's about doing more of the *right things*, for the *right people*, with the *right message*.

If you read the last chapter, you'll remember the importance of tailoring your value propositions to specific buyer personas, because different decision-makers care about different outcomes. That principle doesn't go away when you scale. In fact, it becomes even more important.

One of the biggest mistakes I see when firms try to ramp up outreach is that they lose their focus. They abandon the clarity of persona-driven messaging in favor of generic templates. What started as thoughtful outreach turns into a volume-for-volume's-sake approach, and just like that, all the momentum disappears.

The key to keeping your outreach effective at scale is running multiple, persona-aligned campaigns in parallel. You shouldn't have one campaign that goes to everyone. You should have one for the CFO, one for the Director of Talent Acquisition, one for the VP of Operations, each with messaging built around their specific goals, pain points, and buying triggers.

This might sound complex, but it doesn't have to be. In fact, once you've defined your core personas and written strong messaging tracks for each, you can reuse and refine them over time. You're not starting from scratch with every new campaign; you're *scaling what works* across verticals and roles.

This is a common pivot point I help my clients navigate.
They've built good messaging, but haven't yet structured it into
repeatable, persona-specific campaigns. Once we do that and
layer it into their automation tools, they start seeing consistent
engagement without sacrificing the integrity of their message.

The goal is simple: keep the personal touch, even as you scale the process.

When your outreach is persona-specific, it feels relevant. When it's multi-channel, it feels persistent. And when it's delivered with enough frequency, it gets noticed.

So yes, you need to do more. But you don't need to become someone you're not. You don't need to sound robotic or scripted. You just need to scale the intent you already have with precision.

Because in this market, the firms that break through aren't just louder, they're sharper.

Case Study: Scaling Without Losing the Message

Julian ran a niche staffing firm specializing in compliance roles for financial institutions. His team was small but skilled, and they had recently refined their value proposition: "We help banks reduce regulatory risk by placing compliance talent 50% faster than internal HR." It was clear, relevant, and based on real success.

But Julian hit a wall when trying to scale. His team was sending a couple dozen emails a week, each one manually written. LinkedIn activity was sporadic, and follow-ups were inconsistent. Despite the strong message, outreach volume was too low to move the needle.

We started by building a multi-channel system: automated email sequences, LinkedIn messaging cadences, and structured cold call sprints. Each campaign was tailored to a specific persona—CFOs, Talent Acquisition Leadership, and Hiring Managers—with messaging mapped directly to their concerns: cost savings/audit timelines, time-to-fill rates, and risk mitigation/talent retention.

We used a simple automation tool to schedule and stagger his messages without sacrificing personalization. He didn't blast 1,000 people a day; he ran three highly-targeted, persona-specific campaigns per week, each with 200–300 contacts.

In less than 90 days, the results spoke for themselves: 14 booked meetings, six new clients, and multiple job orders. Just as important, Julian's team felt reenergized. Outreach became a system, not a scramble.

Julian didn't hire more salespeople. He didn't reinvent the wheel. He took a sharp message, paired it with smart systems, and put in the reps.

That's how you scale with precision.

Progress Starts with Push

If this chapter challenged you, that's a good sign. It means you're thinking differently. The truth is, most firms simply aren't doing enough. Not because they're lazy, but because they've never been shown what *enough* actually looks like in today's market.

The game has changed. Buyers are harder to reach. Decisions take longer. Inboxes are noisier. And the firms that win aren't the ones hoping for luck, they're the ones putting in consistent motion with precision and purpose.

You've learned that motion isn't just about more activity, it's about *targeted*, persona-aligned outreach at a scale that gives your message a real shot at breaking through. With the right tools, systems, and discipline, you can dramatically increase your reach without losing your voice.

But volume alone isn't enough. Motion creates momentum, only if you know where it's working.

That's what we're diving into next.

In the next chapter, we'll shift from effort to insight. I'll show you how to measure the outreach you're doing, evaluate what's resonating, and adjust based on the feedback your market is giving you. We'll move from guessing to knowing, from motion to mastery.

Because activity is what starts the engine. But measurement is what keeps it running effectively.

CHAPTER 7

Measure What Matters

"Measure what is measurable,
and make measurable what is not so."
— Galileo Galilei

If you've ever tried to lose weight, build strength, or improve your overall health, you know that guessing doesn't get you very far. The most effective diet and exercise plans all share one thing in common: tracking. You log what you eat. You track your workouts. You watch the numbers, adjust, and stay consistent. Why? Because progress only comes when you can see what's working, and what's not.

Sales is no different.

Too often, I see staffing firms putting in effort but getting frustrated with the results (or lack thereof). They'll say, "We're doing outreach," or "We're talking to prospects," but when I ask how many contacts they made last week, how many conversations led to meetings, or what their conversion rates look like... the answers get fuzzy.

What gets measured gets managed. And what doesn't get measured usually gets repeated, even if it's not working.

This chapter is about building visibility into your sales efforts so you can stop guessing and start optimizing. We're not talking about creating fancy dashboards or burying yourself in spreadsheets. We're talking about tracking the activity that actually drives outcomes and using that data to make smarter, faster decisions.

You don't need perfection. You need consistency. You need clarity. You need a system that shows you what's working, where the gaps are, and what levers to pull to move the numbers.

Let's dig into how we do that and why it's one of the biggest differentiators between firms that simply survive and firms that actually scale.

The Funnel is your Compass

Most people think of the sales funnel as a basic visual, a diagram on a slide that shows how leads become opportunities and eventually become clients. But in my experience, the sales funnel is far more than that. It's not just a diagram, it's a decision-making tool. A compass. A way to guide what happens next.

Every outreach strategy, every messaging change, every adjustment to activity level should be grounded in what your funnel is telling you. If you know where the drop-offs are, you know where the problems are. And if you know where the problems are, you know where to focus your time and energy.

Here's what that looks like in practice:

If you're reaching out to a large number of leads but very few are responding, it's likely a messaging or targeting issue. Your subject lines might not be grabbing attention, or your value proposition isn't resonating with the people you're reaching out to.

If you're getting replies and booking conversations, but those conversations rarely convert to proposals or next steps, the issue may be how you're handling the meetings or whether you're speaking to the right personas.

If you're getting proposals out the door but not closing, that tells you something about your pricing, positioning, or the urgency of the problems you're solving.

Every stage in the funnel is a signal. But you only see those signals if you're paying attention and if you're measuring what happens at each point.

This is one of the first things I do with clients when we build or reboot their sales strategy: we map out the funnel together. Not just to understand the math, but to figure out where the momentum stops. Once we know that, we can fix it — whether it's messaging, motion, targeting, or timing.

The funnel doesn't just show you how many deals you're working. It shows you where your strategy is breaking down and where your biggest opportunities for improvement are hiding.

And when you look at it that way, it becomes more than a chart. It becomes a compass.

You Need More Than One Lens

Most firms are familiar with the concept of a sales funnel, but almost all of them make the same mistake: they treat it like a single, static pipeline. One funnel. One set of metrics. One narrative.

That's a problem.

Because in a well-structured outbound sales strategy, you're not running one campaign, you're running many. Different buyer personas. Different verticals. Different messaging tracks. And the truth is, what's working in one campaign might be falling flat in another. If you only look at the big picture, you'll miss the critical differences that could make or break your results.

This is why I always tell my clients you need more than one funnel.

You need a funnel for each of your targeted campaigns. One for CFOs. One for Directors of Talent Acquisition. One for Operations or HR leaders. Because each of those buyer personas responds to different value propositions, has different sales cycles, and faces different objections.

If you're only looking at one blended funnel, you might think your outreach is underperforming — when in fact, it's just one campaign that's dragging the whole thing down. Or worse, you might think everything's working fine while one of your core personas is completely disengaging and slipping through the cracks.

When I build sales infrastructure for clients, we always create a master funnel — a central dashboard that captures everything, but also allows for filtering. We track activity and conversions by persona, by vertical, by time period, and even by message track when possible. That level of clarity allows for real-time course correction. You're not just measuring, you're learning.

With this setup, a client can quickly see, for example, that their campaign targeting HR leaders in healthcare is generating a 10% response rate, while their outreach to CFOs in manufacturing is producing zero meetings. That insight is gold. It tells us where to double down and where to reevaluate the message or targeting.

The bottom line: you can't optimize what you can't isolate.

Having separate funnels isn't overcomplicating things; it's how you find the signal in the noise. It's how you make smarter decisions faster. And it's how you make sure your strategy isn't just active, it's effective across every audience you serve.

Break It Out, Dial It In

Not every campaign should be treated the same. Some are broad and exploratory, designed to identify potential interest from new segments. Others are more focused, more strategic, and carry a much higher potential for conversion.

One of the highest-leverage campaigns I run for my clients is aimed squarely at the competitors of their current clients.

These prospects aren't just in the same market, they're often facing the exact same challenges our existing clients were struggling with before we helped them. That makes our outreach highly relevant, our messaging sharper, and our credibility stronger. It's not a generic value proposition anymore; it's a proof point with a direct competitive context.

Because of this, I treat these campaigns differently.

When I build a competitor-targeting campaign, I add more steps, more touchpoints, and more channels. I might include a longer sequence of emails, layered with personalized LinkedIn messages, warm call attempts, and in some cases, industry-specific direct mail or gifting.

These are the campaigns where we're not just trying to get noticed, we're trying to make a clear, competitive case. "We helped a firm just like yours solve this problem and here's how." The message hits harder. The engagement tends to be higher. And the stakes are often bigger.

Because this campaign style is so different in cadence, content, and structure, I always run it through a separate sales funnel.

It's not just about visibility, it's about focus. By keeping this campaign's activity, conversions, and deal flow isolated from your standard funnels, you can track its specific performance and optimize it as its own system.

This is especially important because competitor-focused outreach often involves a smaller pool of higher-value prospects. You're not trying to reach hundreds of leads, you're going deep on 10, 20, maybe 30 key companies. So, you need more than raw volume data, you need precision metrics to understand how your efforts are landing with each individual account.

This is a best practice I implement with every client who has a few strong case studies or notable wins: we spin out a high-touch competitor campaign, build a custom sequence around it, and track it separately from everything else. Over time, it becomes a reliable engine for landing strategic, high-fit clients.

If you try to measure a focused campaign like this alongside your broader efforts, the signals get muddied. You miss the nuance. You miss the trends. And you lose the ability to improve what could be your most effective campaign.

The most strategic plays need their own lane and their own funnel.

Case Study: Seeing the Signal, Not Just the Noise

Tanya led a fast-growing staffing firm focused on placing mid-level IT professionals in the insurance sector. Her team was motivated, her messaging was sharp, and outreach volume was solid. But results were mixed. Some weeks were strong, others quiet. Her pipeline felt like a rollercoaster.

When we looked at her metrics, everything was blended. One funnel, one dashboard, one big bucket of activity. That meant her team couldn't isolate what was working from what wasn't.

We broke it out.

First, we separated funnels by persona: one for IT Directors, one for HR, and one for Procurement. Then we created funnels by campaign type: her competitor-focused sequences, her industry-specific campaigns, and a re-engagement track for cold leads.

Immediately, patterns emerged. Her outreach to IT Directors was converting to meetings at nearly 8%, while her HR campaign was under 2%. The competitor-focused campaign had a 25% open rate but was stalling in the proposal stage.

That insight led to clear next steps: we reworked the HR messaging to focus more on candidate experience and time-to-fill, and refined the proposal process for competitor outreach to include customized benchmarks from past successes.

Within 90 days, Tanya's team saw a 40% lift in booked meetings and closed three new accounts. But more importantly, the team had clarity. They weren't just acting, they were adjusting.

That's the power of measuring what matters.

From Prospecting to Partnership

The sales funnel isn't just a visual, it's an essential tool. A way to understand what's working, what's not, and where to adjust. But it only works if you design it to reflect the real structure of your sales strategy, not just one big picture, but multiple views that give you real insight.

That's why you need multiple sales funnels aligned to buyer personas, campaign focus, market verticals, and strategy. Especially when you're running high-touch outreach — like targeting competitors of your current clients — your funnel has to match your intent. The more focused the campaign, the more focused your measurement needs to be.

That level of clarity allows you to stop guessing and start leading. And it completes the foundation of everything we've talked about so far.

Up to this point, we've walked through the **Message. Motion. Measure.** framework — a system for building pipeline in today's tough market. You've clarified your messaging, scaled your outreach, and learned how to track what's working.

Now we shift gears.

Because when that system starts working —when you start generating conversations and booking meetings — you need to be ready for what comes next.

That's where we're headed in Chapter 8.

We'll talk about how to prepare for meetings, how to run them with purpose, and how to show up like the expert your buyer needs.

The prospecting engine is built. Now it's time to deliver.

CHAPTER 8

Meeting the Moment

"Customers don't buy products or services.
They buy better versions of themselves."
— Anonymous

You've done the hard work. You've built your message, increased your motion, and measured what's working. Now the system is doing what it's supposed to do — creating real opportunities.

And this is where a lot of firms stumble.

Because once the meeting gets booked, there's a tendency to shift into autopilot. Maybe it's the confidence of having a strong service. Maybe it's a habit. Maybe it's because we're so used to pitching that we forget to prepare. But either way, too many opportunities are lost in the meeting itself, not because the buyer wasn't interested, but because the seller didn't lead the conversation with intention.

This chapter is about getting that moment right.

We'll start with preparation: what to research, what to bring into the conversation, and what mindset to adopt before you even log in or walk through the door. Then I'll walk you through a simple meeting framework I use to keep conversations focused, consultative, and forward-moving, without slipping into a pitch.

And finally, we'll talk about what buyers are *really* looking for, not just a vendor or a resume-filled inbox, but a partner who helps them become a better, more successful version of themselves.

Because the meeting isn't just a step in the sales process.

It's the moment where trust is built — or lost.

Prep Like a Pro

A booked meeting is not a win; it's an opening. And what you do before that meeting starts often determines how it ends.

The best salespeople don't wing it. They prepare with purpose.

Preparation isn't just about researching the company's website or scanning a LinkedIn profile five minutes before the call. It's about entering the conversation with clarity, confidence, and a plan to lead the buyer where they need to go, even if they don't quite know where that is yet.

Here are the non-negotiables I walk my clients through before every key meeting:

1. Anticipate the Objections

This is one of the most overlooked elements of sales prep. If you've been selling recruiting and staffing services for more than a week, you know what the common objections are. "We already have a vendor." "We're not hiring right now." "We don't use agencies." The mistake isn't being caught off guard, the mistake is *not preparing for what you already know is coming.*

Write down the three to five most likely objections, and script out your responses, not as defensive counterpunches, but as conversation bridges. Be ready to validate concerns, reframe the value, and guide the conversation forward. Confidence matters here.

2. Know Your Client Wins

Buyers don't just want to know what you do, they want to know where it's worked. And they want to hear stories that feel close to home. Before the meeting, identify two to three success stories that are relevant to this buyer's role, industry, or hiring challenge.

Tell them briefly, clearly, and in a way that positions your firm as a capable partner, not a hero. A great story makes your value real and lowers the buyer's perceived risk in working with you.

3. Study the Buyer, Not Just the Company

Yes, review the website. Yes, read the news section. But most of your insight should come from studying the individual. What's their title? What's their likely KPI? What challenges come with that role in their specific industry? Have they posted or commented on LinkedIn recently?

You're not prepping for a pitch; you're prepping for a conversation. And the more you know about who you're talking to, the more likely you are to make it meaningful.

Preparation isn't about scripts. It's about removing guesswork so you can show up and listen, lead, and adapt with confidence.

And the more prepared you are, the more likely you are to earn a next step.

Own the Flow

You wouldn't walk into a job interview, a client kickoff, or a board meeting without a plan — and a sales meeting should be no different.

When it comes to selling recruiting and staffing services, having a framework for your meetings isn't optional; it's essential.

Without a clear structure, it's easy to default into reactive mode: answering their questions, defending your value, or running through a list of services while they mentally check out. That kind of conversation might feel safe, but it rarely leads to meaningful progress and it definitely doesn't position you as a strategic partner.

The best meetings are led — and they're led by the person asking the questions.

A framework doesn't mean you're rigid or scripted. It means you have a clear flow for the conversation — a structure that keeps things focused, opens up the right topics, and helps both you and the buyer discover whether there's a real fit.

> *One of the biggest mindset shifts I coach clients on is this: you're not there to present; you're there to investigate. Your job is to ask thoughtful, targeted questions that uncover real pain points, business goals, and internal pressure points — the things that actually move deals forward.*

A good framework gives you confidence and direction. It ensures that the conversation doesn't get sidetracked into transactional details or turn into a one-sided pitch. It helps you steer the call while keeping the focus on the buyer — their needs, their challenges, their goals.

And it's not just about control; it's about building trust. When you lead the meeting with purpose, it signals that you're prepared, experienced, and worth listening to. You don't need to dominate the call. You just need to own the responsibility of guiding it.

Because a scattered conversation rarely leads to a decision.

But a well-led one? That's what moves the deal.

Sell the Better Version of Them

If there's one truth that reshapes the way you sell, it's this:

Your prospects aren't buying your service. They're buying a better version of themselves.

This mindset shift is at the heart of the meeting framework I help my clients build. While each version is customized to fit their market, team, and strengths, there's one universal principle we never leave out: *the buyer is not only looking for recruiting or staffing. They're looking for a better version of themselves.*

They're looking for smoother operations, less pressure from leadership, fewer fires to put out, and more time to focus on what matters. They're buying peace of mind, internal credibility, efficiency, performance — and in many cases, they're buying a solution that makes them look good.

That's why even a perfectly delivered pitch can fall flat if it's all about you. Your process, your talent pipeline, your differentiators — none of that matters unless it's tied to an outcome they want to see in their own world.

When you show a buyer how your service helps them achieve a transformation — from overworked to in control, from overwhelmed to ahead, from exposed to supported — that's when they start to lean in. That's when trust builds. That's when your service becomes not just relevant, but *essential.*

This is a big reason why your meeting needs to be question-driven, not pitch-driven. You're not just gathering data. You're listening for pain, pressure, and vision. You're finding the gap between where they are and where they want to be, and then helping them see that you can be the bridge.

When I work with clients on this, we build a meeting structure that fits their style but never loses this focus. The goal isn't to close during the meeting, it's to position yourself as the person who understands what's at stake and can help deliver the outcome that matters most to the buyer.

No script can replace that. It comes from asking the right questions, telling the right stories, and making the buyer feel like the decision to work with you is a step toward something better, not just something different.

So yes, you're selling a service. But what they're buying is themselves — just more successful, more confident, and more in control.

Help them see that version. That's how you run the meeting and win the business.

Case Study: Turning a Meeting into Momentum

David ran a ten-person staffing agency specializing in placing project managers in the construction and infrastructure sector. He had recently revamped his outbound strategy and was seeing results: meetings were getting booked, doors were opening. But conversions were inconsistent.

When we reviewed his recent meetings, a pattern emerged: his team was defaulting into pitch mode. They'd rattle off capabilities, list industries served, and talk about their "deep bench of candidates." But they weren't leading the conversation.

We rebuilt their meeting approach from the ground up.

Each rep started using a structured pre-meeting checklist: top three likely objections, two client stories relevant to the buyer's persona, and specific business pain points common to that role. We paired that with a new call framework built around investigative discovery: open-ended questions, role-specific pain, and goal alignment.

David's reps weren't just "taking meetings" anymore. They were leading them.

One rep, Julia, had a call with the VP of Field Operations at a national civil engineering firm. Instead of pitching, she asked about open project timelines, permitting delays, and how their current staffing setup was affecting throughput. The buyer opened up about schedule overruns tied to unfilled PM roles.

Julia walked him through a recent client scenario with almost identical challenges and how they placed three qualified PMs in under 21 days, helping the client stay on track for a critical federal deadline.

The VP scheduled a follow-up for the next morning. Two weeks later, they signed a contract.

The win wasn't because of price, a perfect resume, or a slick deck. It was because the rep ran the meeting like a consultant, not a vendor.

And that's what real trust looks like.

The Foundation Is Set

You've built the system. You've done the outreach. You've booked the meeting. And now you've shown up with purpose, ready to lead a real conversation, not a pitch.

This is where sales gets real. Because the meeting isn't just a checkpoint in your funnel. It's the moment where buyers start to believe. It's where they see what's possible, not just in your service, but in their world if they work with you.

The ability to lead that conversation isn't just a skill but rather a competitive edge.

When you prepare the right way, guide the meeting with intention, and frame your value as the key to your prospect's better future, you do more than earn credibility. You set the stage for real trust and real momentum.

And that momentum builds. Meeting by meeting. Win by win. Campaign by campaign.

In the next chapter, we're going to step back and look at the bigger picture and see what happens when you keep showing up, executing this system, and making small adjustments over time. Because the results don't just add up, they compound.

We'll also talk about what it means to build a sales strategy that endures — one that stays strong no matter what tools, tactics, or tech trends come and go.

Because this isn't about chasing what's new but committing to what works.

CHAPTER 9

The Payoff of Persistence

"I'm convinced that about half of what separates successful entrepreneurs from the non-successful ones is pure perseverance."
— Steve Jobs

You've done the work. You've clarified your message. You've committed to motion. You've put systems in place to measure what matters. You've shown up for meetings with purpose and led conversations that build trust.

You've built a foundation that most staffing and recruiting firms never take the time or make the investment to create.

Now comes the part that's harder to see, but even more powerful: what happens when you stay the course.

Because the real magic in this system isn't just in how it works but also what it builds over time.

Momentum in sales doesn't follow a straight line. It compounds. Small improvements stack. Conversations lead to referrals. Activity creates awareness. Clear messaging travels further than you think. Meetings today become deals tomorrow. It all adds up — quietly and steadily — until suddenly, your pipeline feels predictable, your process feels natural, and your results feel earned.

In this chapter, we'll step back and look at what happens when you continue to show up for the system you've built. We'll talk about the long-term payoff of consistency, the durability of the core principles you've implemented, and why those principles will continue to work — even as tools, trends, and technologies change.

Your future clients aren't looking for the flashiest vendor. They're looking for the firm that shows up, delivers, and keeps improving.

This is where it all comes together and starts working even harder for you.

Let's talk about where this leads.

The Compounding Effect of Consistency

The real value of the system you've built doesn't show up all at once. It builds quietly, gradually — and then, at some point, it starts to snowball.

Because consistency in sales isn't just about staying busy, it's about creating momentum that compounds over time.

At first, you're building from scratch. You're reaching out to a cold market, testing your message, refining your funnels. It's hard work. It can feel repetitive. But every rep is laying a brick. Every conversation is a data point. Every meeting — even if it doesn't turn into business — sharpens your instincts and deepens your understanding of the market.

Then things start to shift.

Your **LinkedIn network expands**. People you spoke with months ago start responding. More of your content gets noticed. You're not just another recruiter or staffing partner showing up; you're someone they've seen, heard from, and started to recognize.

You **win new clients**, and those wins give you new stories — fresh proof points you can weave into future campaigns. You're not pitching possibilities anymore. You're sharing outcomes. That changes how prospects hear you.

Your **reputation grows**, not because you told people how great you are, but because you showed them. You showed up consistently. You followed through. You made their jobs easier, their hiring smoother, and their outcomes stronger.

You **start getting referrals** — sometimes from clients, sometimes from prospects who didn't convert but respected how you showed up. You become known in your niche. Your follow-ups land better. Your close rates improve, not because your pitch changed, but because you've earned more credibility just by staying the course.

This is what I tell every client who feels like the results are taking longer than expected: You're not only building a pipeline, but you're also building a presence. And once that presence is established, everything gets easier.

What starts out feeling manual becomes more efficient. Your campaigns get sharper. Your messaging gets tighter. Your targeting gets cleaner. You know what works, and more importantly, you know *why* it works.

But none of that happens if you stop. None of it happens if you change course every month. None of it happens if you're chasing new tools instead of doubling down on what you've already built.

Consistency compounds. That's the truth most people ignore and the edge you now have.

Principles Over Platforms

Technology changes. Tools evolve. AI is rewriting parts of how we work, prospect, and even communicate. But here's the truth that often gets lost in the noise:

The principles don't change.

The most effective sales systems — the kind you've been building throughout this book — are rooted in strategy, not software. They're built on clarity of message, consistent motion, smart measurement, and meaningful conversations. These aren't trends. These are the fundamentals. And they've worked across industries, across market cycles, and across generations of sales tools.

Yes, AI is changing the game. There are tools now that can draft outreach messages, generate lists, transcribe meetings, and even help analyze buyer intent. Used well, these tools are powerful. But they're accelerators, not replacements. They don't eliminate the need for a system. They enhance it.

That's what I show my clients: how to integrate AI and automation into their workflow without losing control of the process. We find ways to scale outreach faster, track insights more efficiently, and personalize messaging with less manual effort, all while staying true to the core principles that make the strategy work in the first place.

The real danger isn't AI. It's distraction. I've worked with business owners who spent weeks chasing new platforms, new plug-ins, or new "shortcut" tools. By the time we started working together, they had burned time, energy, and budget, and still had no consistent system for generating new business.

They weren't wrong to experiment. But they skipped the foundation. They tried to automate what they hadn't first built.

And here's the truth: If they had invested that same time into building a proven, principle-based system for attracting and converting clients — the kind you've been learning chapter by chapter — they'd be far ahead of where they are now.

That's why this process isn't about resisting change. It's about anchoring your business to a strategy that's strong enough to adapt, no matter what tool, trend, or tech wave comes next.

Because clarity, consistency, and credibility never go out of style.

And when you start there, everything else becomes easier to plug in.

From Strategy to Execution

Everything you've built to this point — the message, the motion, the metrics, the meetings — it's not theory. It's not a guess. It's a system rooted in the same principles that top-performing sales teams in the recruiting and staffing industry are already using to win business, grow accounts, and stay consistent through tough markets.

This isn't about doing what's trendy. It's about doing what works and doing it well, over time.

If you stick with this process, if you keep showing up and making small improvements, the compounding will kick in. The system will start to pay you back. And what once felt heavy will start to feel automatic.

That's how growth becomes sustainable — not from hacks or shortcuts, but from building something that lasts.

But before we close this out, there's one more thing I want to give you: a reality check.

Because even with the right system, implementation can go sideways. I've seen it happen. In the next chapter, I'm going to walk you through the most common mistakes firms make when trying to put this system into practice — and I'll share what it really takes in tools, time, and team, to make it work.

You've got the framework. Now let's make sure you avoid the pitfalls.

CHAPTER 10

Beyond the Blueprint

"You don't have to be great to start,
but you have to start to be great."
— Zig Ziglar

You've made it to the final chapter and by now, you've done more than just read about a system. You've started to see how it all connects. You've learned how top-performing staffing and recruiting firms clarify their message, scale their motion, measure what matters, and lead conversations that build real trust.

You've built the strategy. Now it's time to implement it.

And this is where things often go sideways.

It's not because the strategy is flawed. It's because execution is where most good ideas get lost. Between the day-to-day pressures of running a business and the complexity of building out a system, it's easy to fall into partial implementation, get stuck chasing shiny tools, or lose steam when the results aren't immediate.

This final chapter is designed to help you avoid those traps.

We'll start by looking at the most common mistakes I see when firms try to put this system into place — and what to do instead. Then we'll walk through the tools you'll need to support this process: what's essential, what's optional, and what I use with my clients to keep things moving efficiently. Finally, we'll talk about time and how much of it this takes, how to approach it with realistic expectations, and how to know whether you should implement this internally or bring in outside support.

Because you've come too far to stop short now. Let's make sure you execute this the right way.

Common Mistakes

The system you've built throughout this book is simple but that doesn't make it easy. And while the components are straightforward, I've seen even smart, capable teams stall out in implementation because of a handful of avoidable missteps.

Let's talk about them so you can avoid them.

1. Weak or Generic Value Propositions

The first and most foundational mistake is failing to develop strong, buyer-specific value propositions. Too often, firms rely on vague claims like "great talent" or "fast service," which do little to differentiate them from the sea of competitors saying the exact same thing.

When I work with clients, we use specific templates I've developed to extract real messaging from the success stories and outcomes they've already created. The goal is to move from what we do to how we've helped, so we can speak directly to what the buyer values most, not just what we're proud of.

2. A CRM That Doesn't Show You Anything

The second mistake is not configuring your CRM to give you visibility into your own sales activity. I often find clients using a CRM like a glorified contact list with no structure, no reporting, no way to measure effort or outcomes.

If your CRM can't show you how many calls were made, how many emails were sent, and how many conversations were booked, and to *whom*, then it's not helping you run your business. It's just a database.

3. Letting the Funnel Collect Dust

Your sales funnel isn't something you check in on once a quarter. It's a living system that needs to be reviewed, questioned, and adjusted weekly. When clients start updating their funnel consistently, segmenting it by persona, reviewing conversion rates, and watching for stuck deals — that's when everything starts to click.

Without that rhythm, the system loses momentum. Small issues compound. And opportunities slip through the cracks.

4. Half-Hearted Implementation

The most damaging mistake I see? Starting strong, then pulling back too soon. This usually happens when early outreach doesn't lead to immediate results. Doubt creeps in, the team gets distracted, and the system is quietly abandoned in favor of old habits.

The truth is, this strategy works only if you give it enough time to work. That doesn't mean waiting forever; it means giving it a real window of consistent effort before making big changes.

The clients who see the best results are the ones who go all-in. They commit to the process. They don't try to reinvent it halfway through. They let the system do what it's designed to do and it pays off.

These mistakes are common but they're avoidable.

Simple Stack. Smart Strategy.

One of the most common misconceptions I hear from business owners is that they think they need a massive tech stack to run a modern outbound sales strategy. A half-dozen integrations, complicated dashboards, AI overlays, and every shiny sales tool that shows up in their feed.

Let me be clear: you don't need a mountain of tools. You need a small, focused set and you need to use them well.

Here's what I recommend, and what I help my clients implement:

A CRM You'll Actually Use

The CRM is your sales operating system. It doesn't need to be expensive or flashy; it just needs to give you clear visibility into your pipeline and activity. You should be able to see contacts, outreach history, meeting outcomes, and deal stages all in one place.

More importantly, your CRM should be configured to support the way *you* sell. That means it's structured to reflect your buyer personas, your funnels, and your campaign tracking. This is what I help clients set up from day one — because a CRM that's too basic or too bloated gets ignored. And when it's ignored, so is the data that drives decisions.

LinkedIn Sales Navigator

If you're serious about targeting the right buyers, LinkedIn Sales Navigator is essential. It gives you advanced filters, better lead tracking, and insight into what your prospects are talking about — all of which help you build smarter, more relevant campaigns.

It's also where a lot of your early-stage engagement will happen. Many of the first touches in your outreach sequences will come through LinkedIn. With Sales Navigator, you'll have the tools to make that outreach more focused and more efficient.

A Campaign Automation Tool

You don't need five automation tools. You need one that helps you run multi-touch campaigns across LinkedIn and email. The goal isn't mass outreach. It's **consistent, persona-specific, well-paced sequences** that run in the background while you focus on conversations.

There are several tools that work well here (and I help clients pick the right one based on their workflow), but the key is that it integrates with your CRM, allows for personalization at scale, and gives you visibility into connection rates, replies, and engagement.

The only major campaign I don't fully automate is the client-competitor campaign I mentioned earlier. That one gets a little more hands-on attention, and usually deserves its own dedicated track.

That's it. No bloat. No complexity. Just the essentials used with intention.

And once these tools are set up and aligned with your strategy, everything else becomes easier to manage, scale, and improve.

Time, Commitment, and When to Get Help

If you've made it this far, you know this isn't a "quick fix" system. It's not built on hacks or shortcuts. It's a repeatable, proven strategy — and like anything that produces real, lasting results, it takes time, focus, and consistency to execute well.

That doesn't mean it's complicated. It means it's a commitment.

Once your tools are in place and your messaging is built, the system can be run in a lean, focused way. But getting to that point takes a dedicated stretch of time and attention. It takes leadership. It takes process. And it takes someone who's willing to champion the system, not just build it and hope it runs.

That's where I've seen firms struggle.

They assign implementation to someone already stretched thin. They rush through the value proposition work. They skip persona targeting and jump into campaigns too quickly. Or they stop after a few weeks when the pipeline doesn't explode immediately. The truth is, I've seen this system produce serious results, but never without real commitment.

So what does it actually take?

In most cases, my clients spend the first 4–6 weeks working directly with me to build the messaging, set up the tools, and launch the first few campaigns. Over the next few weeks, we collaborate to configure the CRM, create the initial funnels, and fine-tune the automation cadence. From there, we set a rhythm for outreach, measurement, and optimization.

And while some teams continue running the system themselves, others choose to keep me involved to coach the team, refine the process, and make sure the momentum never stalls.

You can build and run this system on your own. Everything in this book has been designed to give you the roadmap. But if you want help making it happen faster — with fewer false starts and more confidence — that's what I do every day.

The goal isn't to create more work. It's to create more results and fewer wasted cycles getting there.

But in either case, you've done the hard part:

You've learned the system.

Now it's time to decide how you'll bring it to life.

CONCLUSION

Reading a book won't change your business. Taking action will.

By now, you've seen how the top-performing staffing and recruiting firms operate differently. They don't rely on outdated tactics or one-off campaigns. They don't hope for referrals. They build a sales engine — one based on clear messaging, consistent activity, measurable funnels, and conversations that convert.

You have that blueprint now.

But a strategy is only as good as your willingness to implement it. It's easy to let momentum fade once the pages stop turning. The real challenge and the real opportunity is what you do *next*.

Most firms never take that next step. They keep chasing what's comfortable or familiar. They launch one campaign, then pull back when it doesn't land right away. They get distracted by the next tool, the next fire, or the next excuse.

But if you've read this far, you're not like most firms. You've seen what it takes. You've got the roadmap. Now it's about doing the work or bringing in the help you need to make it happen.

Because action — sustained, strategic action — is what separates struggling firms from scaling firms. You don't need to be perfect. You just need to start.

Imagine your calendar filling with qualified meetings — the kind of conversations you actually want to have — with companies who've already started to see you as a partner, not just a vendor.

Imagine waking up with clarity — knowing who your team is targeting, seeing your outreach campaigns run in the background, watching your sales funnel show real movement. Not noise. Not clutter. But momentum.

You're no longer guessing. You're no longer relying on random referrals or old relationships to keep your business moving. You're building new opportunities — on purpose — every week.

And you're not doing more just to stay busy; you're doing the *right* things, consistently.

Over time, your messaging sharpens. Your outreach becomes second nature. Your meetings convert faster. Your reputation grows. You land more of the clients you want, and fewer clients who burn time and budget.

This isn't about becoming a salesperson but rather about becoming a leader — one who owns the revenue side of the business as confidently as the delivery side.

Because once your sales process becomes reliable, everything else gets easier. You can hire with more confidence, forecast with more accuracy, and focus more of your time on what actually matters.

That's what this system builds. That's what your future can look like if you stick with it.

There's no neutral in this market. You're either moving forward, or slowly falling behind.

The firms that hesitate — the ones that stay stuck in outdated habits or wait for things to "settle down" — are the ones watching competitors pass them by. Not because they weren't capable, but because they didn't act.

The risk of inaction is more than missed revenue. It's missed momentum. It's watching new opportunities slip away while old ones dry up. It's feeling stuck, even when you know you should be further along.

And the longer you wait, the harder it gets. The more outdated your systems feel. The harder it becomes to make a change. The more frustrated your team gets. And the more your confidence slips.

Meanwhile, the firms that commit — even imperfectly — are already building. They're reaching the right people. They're learning what works. They're gaining ground you haven't started claiming yet.

You've already done the hard part: you've invested the time to learn the system. The real risk now is letting it sit on a shelf.

Implement it. Lead your team. Or, if you want help getting it right, let's talk. That's what I do every day for firms just like yours.

If you would like to explore the impact this system can make for your business and how I can help you implement it, you can schedule an exploratory call on my website at www.salesfireconsulting.com or you can email me directly at brian.lile@salesfireconsulting.com.

Because growth doesn't happen on its own. And your next chapter won't write itself.